11+
Verbal Reasoning
CEM Style

WORKBOOK **1**

Verbal Ability Technique

Dr Stephen C Curran

with Katrina MacKay & Autumn McMahon

Edited by Andrea Richardson

This book belongs to

ae
TUITION

Accelerated Education Publications Ltd

Contents

Chapter One
CLASSIFICATION

Classification involves working out the meanings of words. Once the meanings of the words have been understood, they can be separated into their correct groupings. This applies to any form of grouping, including all objects, meanings of words, ideas and subject areas.

An example of a simple classification (grouping) of animals:
- mammals have hair or fur (e.g. cat, horse)
- reptiles have scales (e.g. alligator, snake)
- birds have feathers and wings (e.g. eagle, sparrow)
- amphibians live on land and in water (e.g. frog, toad)
- fish breathe underwater using gills (e.g. shark, salmon)

Work connected with classification requires excellent spelling and vocabulary skills. Working through the Spelling & Vocabulary workbooks will develop these skills.

The following question types involve classification:

Odd One Out • Synonyms • Antonyms • Homonyms

1. Odd One Out

Odd One Out involves finding the word that does not belong to the group. This is done by deciding what the particular grouping is and which word does not fit into this grouping. There are a number of different types of odd one out question:

Noun Grouping • Word Play • Word Meanings

a. Noun Grouping

This type of Odd One Out question is about deciding on the group a noun might belong to. A noun is a name for a person, place or thing, e.g. oboe, flute, piccolo, clarinet and bassoon are all names of wind instruments.

Exercise 1: 1   Underline the odd one out:

1) slippers   trousers   sandals   trainers   boots
2) king   prince   waiter   nephew   aunt
3) chicken   rhino   elephant   giraffe   zebra
4) daisy   daffodil   oak   tulip   rose
5) library   classroom   kitchen   lounge   hotel
6) rugby   tennis   football   cricket   ball
7) England   London   Ireland   Scotland   Wales
8) teacher   litter   flock   clutch   herd
9) yoghurt   juice   lemonade   squash   smoothie
10) pen   pencil   paper   crayon   chalk

Record scores out of ten here
↓

b. Word Play

This type of Odd One Out question is about how words are put together, not what the words mean. It includes the following types:

- Matching Letters – a group of words that contain the same letters or combinations of letters, e.g. flee<u>ing</u> and buy<u>ing</u>
- Palindromes – words that read the same forwards and backwards, e.g. madam
- Rhyming Words – words that have the same sound or end with the same sound, e.g. note and boat
- Silent Letters – words that contain letters that are not sounded when they are spoken, e.g. dum<u>b</u> and <u>g</u>naw
- Semordnilaps – words that will spell another word backwards, e.g. tip spells pit backwards

Exercise 1: 2   Underline the odd one out:

1) slow   row   <u>echo</u>   bow   allow

2) scales   scarecrow   seagull   scratch   scaffold

3) pup   rear   bib   eye   wow

4) wrapper   wrong   wrestle   right   wrist

5) ring   amazing   sing   join   fling

6) table   shovel   bubble   tumble   prickle

7) raw   top   met   lap   ton

8) him   time   rhyme   climb   mime

9) smart   sheet   shirt   snout   slate

10) man   net   pit   tap   nip

Score

c. Word Meanings

In this type of Odd One Out question all but one of the words have similar meanings (synonyms).

For example, funny, humorous, comical, hilarious and hysterical all have similar meanings.

Exercise 1: 3   Underline the odd one out:

1) small   size   little   tiny   minute
2) good   stupid   silly   idiotic   foolish
3) mad   crazy   insane   frantic   calm
4) laugh   giggle   frown   chuckle   cackle
5) hot   boiling   burning   close   warm
6) damp   soaking   fine   watery   dripping
7) ancient   new   worn   wrinkled   old
8) surprise   astonish   shock   amaze   great
9) nice   evil   wicked   horrid   nasty
10) upset   miserable   unhappy   glad   sad

d. Mixed Examples

Exercise 1: 4   Underline the odd one out:

1) cry   weep   sob   wail   sad
2) but   wed   pink   flow   paws
3) red   yellow   green   blue   sky
4) outside   centre   middle   inside   inner
5) under   beneath   below   bellow   underneath

6) [Sun] Jupiter Mars Venus Earth

7) hobby [cry] bee three story

8) burger sandwich crisps [water] apple

9) pool snip (thin) star stew

10) maid (meat) (march) market (make

Score

2. Synonyms

A **Synonym** is a word that has a similar meaning to another word. There are two types of synonym question:

Select the Synonym • **Spell the Synonym**

a. Select the Synonym

Example:

> Which one of the following words is a synonym of the word **spin**?
>
> **look   around   turn   behind**

1. Try to decide the meaning of the key word. **Spin** means to rotate or whirl around quickly.

2. Compare the meanings of each word with **spin**.

   • **look** means to see something or how something appears.

   • **around** means to turn the other way or travel on the outside of something.

   • **behind** means to be located at the back of.

3. Only **turn** remains. **Turn** means to change position by rotating. This word is similar in meaning to **spin**.

4. Check if both words fit into the same sentence.

   'The person spins around.' 'The person turns around.' Both of these words work in this sentence.

   The correct synonym is: turn

Exercise 1: 5

Underline the word which is a synonym of the word in bold:

1) **beginning**   end   finish   ~~start~~   bringing

2) **cover**   ~~hide~~   seek   find   look

3) **rock**   roll   ~~stone~~   ages   wall

4) **rest**   busy   calm   chaos   ~~relax~~

5) **couch**   chair   ~~sofa~~   bed   stool

6) **add**   subtract   more   extra   ~~plus~~

7) **dark**   light   cloudy   ~~shady~~   night

8) **grin**   ~~smile~~   frown   laugh   cry

9) **kind**   enjoy   ~~caring~~   healthy   awful

10) **mucky**   ~~dirty~~   clean   wet   dry

b. Spell the Synonym

Example: Complete the word on the right by filling in the missing letters. It is a synonym of the word on the left.

spoke		t		l		e	d

1. Think about the word on the left and its meaning. **Spoke** can mean to have said something or a part of a wheel. Now look for a word that has a similar meaning on the right. This clue may give the missing word straight away but, if not, proceed to the next step.

2. Normally there is a vowel after the first letter in most words, so it is likely to be either **a**, **e**, **i**, **o** or **u**. The letter **a** gives the most options in this word.

3. Try out letters from the alphabet in the second space. The letter **l** can only be followed by certain letters in a word. Some common patterns are **ld**, **lk**, **lm**, **lt** and **ly**. These letters could be tried out.

t	a	l	d	e	d
t	a	l	k	e	d
t	a	l	m	e	d
t	a	l	t	e	d
t	a	l	y	e	d

4. It is now fairly easy to spot the word as none of the other possibilities spells a proper word. The word **talked** means to have said something, so it fits the given clue.

The correct synonym is: talked

Exercise 1: 6

Complete the word on the right by filling in the missing letters. It is a synonym of the word on the left:

1) **bar**

p	o	l	e

2) **thin**

n	a	r	r	o	w

3) **blank**

E	m	p	t	y

4) **afraid**

s	c	a	r	e	d

5) **stay**

r	e	m	a	i	n

6) **bunny**

r	a	b	b	i	t

7) **correct**

r	i	g	h	t

8) **seaside**

b	e	a	c	h

9) **cold** | c | h | i | l | l | y

10) **each** | e | v | e | r | y

Score

c. Mixed Examples

Exercise 1: 7

Complete or underline the word on the right that is a synonym of the word on the left:

1) **near**   under   over   close   away

2) **pretty**   ugly   tall   beautiful   short

3) **slam**   quiet   bang   miss   creak

4) **each**   again   just   every   any

5) **core**   outer   inside   centre   apple

6) **mute**   s | i | l | e | n | t

7) **kind**   h | e | l | p | f | u | l

8) **fast**   q | u | i | c | k

9) **rush**   h | u | r | r | y

10) **great**   f | a | n | t | a | s | t | i | c

Score

3. Antonyms

An **Antonym** is a word that is opposite in meaning to another word. There are two types of antonym question:

Select the Antonym • **Spell the Antonym**

a. Select the Antonym

Example: | Which one of the following words is an antonym of the word **small**?
tiny   little   big   mini

1. Try to decide the meaning of the key word. **Small** means of limited size or not large.
2. Compare the meanings of each word with **small**.
   - **tiny** means minute and is similar in meaning to **small** (synonym), but the question asks for an opposite meaning (antonym).
   - **little** means not big and is a synonym of **small**.
   - **mini** means of reduced size and is a synonym of **small**.
3. Only **big** remains. **Big** means large. This is the opposite of **small** and looks like the correct answer.
4. Check if both words fit into the same sentence.
   'The house is small.' 'The house is big.'
   Both of these words work in this sentence, and the meaning changes to its opposite.

The correct antonym is: big

Exercise 1: 8

Underline the word which is an antonym of the word in bold:

Score

1) **yell**   shout   whisper   scream   bellow

2) **ill**   sick   unwell   well   poorly

3) **boy**   male   man   guy   girl

4) **under**   beneath   over   below   between

5) **clean**   neat   dirty   tidy   clear

---

6) **East**   North ⟦West⟧ up down

7) **high**   ⟦low⟧ raise up tall

8) **before**   next between ⟦after⟧ behind

9) **cry**   weep wail sob ⟦laugh⟧

10) **pass**   correct ⟦fail⟧ right wrong

b. Spell the Antonym

Example: Complete the word on the right by filling in the missing letters. It is an antonym of the word on the left.

rare

c		m		o	n

1. Think about the word on the left and its meaning. **Rare** means unusual. Now look for a word that has the opposite meaning on the right.

   This clue may give the missing word straight away but, if not, proceed to the next step.

2. Try out letters from the alphabet in the first space. Only a vowel will fit between the letters **c** and **m**. Try out the different options; **a**, **e**, **i**, **o** and **u**.

c	a	m		o	n
c	e	m		o	n
c	i	m		o	n
c	o	m		o	n
c	u	m		o	n

If this does not give the word then move on.

3. Try out letters from the alphabet in the other space where only a few letters could possibly fit. Two possibilities are **m** and **p**.

c	a	m	m	o	n
c	e	m	m	o	n
c	i	m	m	o	n
c	o	m	m	o	n
c	u	m	m	o	n

c	a	m	p	o	n
c	e	m	p	o	n
c	i	m	p	o	n
c	o	m	p	o	n
c	u	m	p	o	n

4. It is now fairly easy to spot the word as all the other possibilities do not spell proper words. The word **common** refers to an object that is ordinary or an activity that is done often, which is the opposite of **rare**.

The correct antonym is: common

Exercise 1: 9

Complete the word on the right by filling in the missing letters. It is an antonym of the word on the left:

1) **dark**　　　| l | i | g | h | t |

2) **add**　　　| s | u | b | t | r | a | c | t |

3) **big**　　　| l | i | t | t | l | e |

4) **listen**　　| s | p | e | a | k |

5) **alive**　　| d | e | a | d |

6) **worse**　　| b | e | t | t | e | r |

7) **late**　　　| e | a | r | l | y |

8) **jolly** | u p s e t |

9) **false** | t r u e |

10) **nothing** | e v e r y t h i n g |

Score

c. Mixed Examples

Exercise 1: 10 Complete or underline the word on the right that is an antonym of the word on the left:

1) **right**   up   down   left   side

2) **last**   next   first   previous   place

3) **inside**   inner   middle   centre   outside

4) **quiet**   silent   loud   still   calm

5) **strong**   weak   week   powerful   tough

6) **arrive** | l e a v e |

7) **open** | c l o s e d |

8) **day** | n i g h t |

9) **raw** | c o o k e d |

10) **end** | s t a r t |

Score

14   © 2017 Stephen Curran

4. Homonyms

Homonyms are words that have the same spelling, but have different meanings.

Example: | Which word will go equally well with both sets of words in the brackets?
(difficult, tough)   (solid, firm)
strong   hard   thick   stiff

One of these words is a homonym (has more than one meaning) and will match both sets of words in the brackets.

1. Think about the meanings of the words in each set of brackets and decide the difference between them.

(difficult, tough)

Difficult and **tough** describe things that are not easy.

(solid, firm)

Solid and **firm** mean something is securely fixed in place.

2. Now check the meaning of each word in turn to see if it matches either of the sets of words in the brackets:

- **Strong** means something that is hard to break or being powerful. However, this does not fit with **difficult**.

- **Thick** can refer to a liquid that is hard to stir, but does not mean **solid**.

- **Stiff** means something that is hard to move. It does match **firm** but it does not mean **tough**.

- Only **hard** remains. **Hard** can mean not easy or **difficult** and it can also mean something that will not move and is firmly fixed in place. This is the correct answer as it matches both meanings.

The correct homonym is: hard

Exercise 1: 11

Underline the one word which will link the two pairs of bracketed words:

1) (hands, bodies)
   (gun, sword)

   cannon   legs   arms   elbows

2) (dance, disco)
   (sphere, globe)

   sport   ball   spin   tango

3) (yelp, woof)
   (skin, wood)

   bark   tree   trunk   howl

4) (loop, knot)
   (bob, curtsy)

   nod   arch   ribbon   bow

5) (cry, weep)
   (rip, shred)

   tear   snag   grab   wail

6) (quick, speedy)
   (secure, closed)

   shut   fast   safe   swift

7) (group, orchestra)
   (rubber, elastic)

   star   band   pencil   song

8) (first, third)
   (minute, hour)

   place   day   second   last

9) (banner, symbol)
   (mark, label)

   tick   barrier   flag   pick

10) (fight, spar)
    (case, chest)

    trunk   box   hit   punch

Score

Chapter Two
CLOZE

Cloze exercises involve filling in missing words or parts of words that have been taken out of a passage of text. Cloze questions involve understanding the context (the words that surround the word) and vocabulary in order to find the correct words or part of a word that needs to be filled in.

Parts of Speech

It is important when doing a cloze activity to understand parts of speech as this can often help in finding missing words. A part of speech describes what a word does in the sentence. Many words work as different parts of speech depending on how they are used in a sentence.

For example:
David wanted to **train** (verb) to operate a locomotive so he could join a **train** (adjective) company and drive a **train** (noun) every day.

- Nouns – the name of a person, place or thing, e.g. **spoon**

- Adjective – a word that describes a noun, e.g. **soup** spoon

- Verb – a 'doing' word that shows activity, e.g. **ran**

- Adverb – a word that describes a verb, e.g. ran **fast**

- Conjunction or Connective – a joining word that links two parts of a sentence, e.g. **and** or **but**

- Preposition – a word showing how words relate to each other. It can be thought of as showing position in time or space, e.g. came **after** dinner
- Pronoun – a word that replaces a noun, e.g. **he** or **them**

Context

Look at the meaning of the passage in which the missing word or word with missing letters is situated, as this can offer clues to solving cloze questions.

There are three types of cloze test:

Multiple-choice • **Word Bank** • **Missing Letters**

1. Multiple-choice

In **Multiple-choice** style questions there are three possibilities for each missing word in the cloze passage.

Example: Read the following cloze passage and identify the missing word from each multiple-choice option.

Breakfast is said to be the (**1.** most, least, often)

important meal of the (**2.** week, month, day).

The most (**3.** common, rare, often) things to

(**4.** drink, eat, sleep) for breakfast

(**5.** is, are, was) toast and cereal.

1. Read the whole passage and try and decide what it is about, as this will provide clues for each missing word.

This passage describes the morning meal of breakfast. The following method applies to all five questions but the following just looks at questions 1 and 2:

Breakfast is said to be the (**1.** most, least, often) important meal of the (**2.** week, month, day).

2. Leave aside any words that do not fit in the sentence.

Breakfast is said to be the **often** important meal of the **month**.

Neither **often** nor **month** work in questions 1 and 2 as **often** cannot have 'the' in front of it in the sentence. Also, meals are eaten every day and not each month.

3. Check for any words that do not fit the meaning.

Breakfast is said to be the **least** important meal of the **week**.

Neither **least** nor **week** work in questions 1 and 2 as breakfast is a very important meal. Also, meals are eaten every day and not once a week.

4. Try the remaining words in the sentence and see if they work.

Breakfast is said to be the **most** important meal of the **day**.

Both these words work in the sentence. The answers are: **1. most 2. day**

Following the same method the other questions will give the following answers: **3. common 4. eat 5. are**

Exercise 2: 1

Underline the correct words to complete the sentence:

1) The thunderstorms (yesterday, tomorrow, Tuesday) were very (dry, loud, quiet) with lots of (dark, rain, light) flashes.

2) The clowns at the (zoo, circus, moon) were very (funny, lost, anger) and squirted (jelly, sugar, water) over the audience.

3) Big Ben is the (word, work, name) used for the bell of a (clock, house, palace) in London, (Ireland, England, Wales).

4) Sandwiches are made by putting (sand, water, filling) between two (slices, loaves, packs) of bread and they are often (drunk, eaten, thrown) at lunchtime.

5) The (child, dog, fish) felt (happy, ill, sad) and so went to see the (pilot, vent, doctor).

6) The (ship, pirate, parrot) followed the (map, sea, land) to find the (town, water, treasure).

7) There was a lot of (leaves, lightning, rain) yesterday and today there are floods on the (train, car, van) tracks, causing (late, delays, early).

8) The red (dog, bird, kite) is a (smallest, large, tiny) bird of (prey, pray, grey).

9) Scafell Pike is the (lowest, highest, middle) mountain in England, (located, left, made) in the Lake District; it is 978 metres (below, on, above) sea level.

10) Fairy tales are (non-fictional, fictional, myth) stories that are designed for (adults, dogs, children) and are usually about a (princess, frogs, dog).

Cloze passages include various forms of text:
Historical • Biographical
General Knowledge • Literary Text Prose

a. Literary Text Prose

Score

Exercise 2: 2
Select the correct words to complete the passage:

"Humph!" said the Camel.

"I shouldn't say that **1)**
☑ again
☐ repeat
☐ often
if I were you," said the Djinn;

"you might say it once **2)**
☐ to
☐ two
☐ too
often. I want you to work."

And the Camel **3)**

- [ ] slept
- [x] said
- [ ] say

, "Humph!" again; but no

4)
- [x] sooner
- [ ] slower
- [ ] fast

had he said it than he saw his back, that he was

so **5)**
- [x] proud
- [ ] happy
- [ ] sad

of, puffing up and puffing up into a great

6)
- [ ] small
- [x] big
- [ ] medium

lolloping humph.

"Do you **7)**
- [x] see
- [ ] felt
- [ ] touch

that?" said the Djinn. "That's your very

own humph that you've brought upon your very own self by not

8)
- [ ] drinking
- [ ] eating
- [x] working

. Today is Thursday, you've done no work

since Monday, when the work **9)**
- [x] began
- [ ] begin
- [ ] start

. Now you are

10)
- [ ] doing
- [x] going
- [ ] need

to work."

An extract from *Just So Stories* by Rudyard Kipling (1865-1936).

b. Biographical

Exercise 2: 3

Select the correct words to complete the passage:

George Stephenson is **1)**
- ☑ known
- ☐ named
- ☐ fame

for building steam trains,

known as locomotives, for the first railways. He **2)**
- ☐ talked
- ☑ learnt
- ☐ worked

about **3)**
- ☐ wooden
- ☑ coal
- ☑ steam

engines by helping his father. George started

4)
- ☑ working
- ☐ school
- ☐ teaching

from the age of 8 and did not go to school. At 14,

George wanted to read, **5)**
- ☐ rite
- ☐ right
- ☑ write

and count, so that he could

get a better job, so he went to school three nights a week

6)
- ☑ after
- ☐ before
- ☐ between

work. He built his **7)**
- ☐ seven
- ☑ first
- ☐ little

train in 1814.

There was a competition to find the **8)**
- ☑ best
- ☐ fast
- ☐ good

locomotive,

with a pize of £500. Stephenson entered with his

9)
| ☐ toy |
| ☑ train |
| ☐ car |

called the 'Rocket'. It travelled 10)

| ☑ faster |
| ☐ slower |
| ☐ quickly |

than the others and did not break down, so he won the contest.

2. Word Bank

In **Word Bank** style questions there are a number of possible missing words at the top of the page. Words are chosen from this word bank to fill the spaces in the passage.

Example: Choose the correct words from the word bank to fill each space in the cloze passage.

| England | Kingdom | Europe |
| city | four | |

The United 1) _Kingdom_ is made up of
2) _four_ countries: Northern Ireland,
Scotland, Wales and England. The capital
3) _city_ is London, which is in 4) _England_.
The state is in 5) _Europe_.

1. Read the whole passage and decide what the passage is about as this will provide clues for the missing words. This passage gives facts about the United Kingdom.

2. Take each word in turn and try and establish its part of speech and meaning:

- **England** is a proper noun and the name of a country.
- **Kingdom** is a proper noun and means an area ruled by a king or queen.
- **Europe** is a proper noun and is a continent.
- **city** is a noun that means a large town.
- **four** could be a noun or adjective and it is a number.

3. Examine each cloze space and look for clues in the text that might help you find the correct word from the bank:

- 'United _____ is' – The capital letter shows a proper noun. There are three choices: **England** and **Europe** are possible, but **Kingdom** seems more likely as the United Kingdom is a country.

- 'of _____ countries' – This must be an adjective. The only adjective option is **four**.

- 'capital _____ is London' – This must be a noun. The only noun option is **city**, and London is a city.

- 'London, which is in _____' – The word 'in' suggests a place, which is a proper noun. There are two options, **Europe** or **England**. England seems more likely as London is a city and England is a country.

- 'the state is in _____' – The only word left is **Europe**.

The passage would therefore read:

The United **Kingdom** is made up of **four** countries: Northern Ireland, Scotland, Wales and England. The capital **city** is London, which is in **England**. The state is in **Europe**.

a. Literary Text Prose

Exercise 2: 4

Choose the correct words from the word bank to complete the passage below:

still	narrow	middle	boat	lay
courage	swam	fish	full	sink

The paper **1)** _Boat_ parted in the **2)** _Middle_,

and the Soldier was about to **3)** _Sink_, when he was

swallowed by a great **4)** _Fish_.

Oh, how dark it was! Darker even than in the drain, and so

5) _narrow_ but the Tin Soldier kept his **6)** _courage_,

there he **7)** _Swam_ at **8)** _full_ length, shouldering

his gun as before.

To and fro **9)** _lay_ the fish, turning and twisting

and making the strangest movements, till at last he became

perfectly **10)** _Still_.

An extract from *The Steadfast Tin Soldier* by Hans Christian Andersen (1805-1875).

b. General Knowledge

Exercise 2: 5

Choose the correct words from the word bank to complete the passage below:

capital	largest	colours	six	world
city	Reef	country	many	two

Australia is a **1)** _Country_ that is divided into

2) _six_ states: Southern Australia, Western Australia,

New South Wales, Queensland, Victoria and Tasmania; and

3) _two_ territories: Northern Territory and Australian

Capital Territory. The capital **4)** _city_ of Australia is

Canberra, however **5)** _many_ people get confused and

say that Sydney is the **6)** _Capital_. The national symbols

of Australia are: a flower called the Golden Wattle, a gemstone

called opal and two **7)** _Colours_ – green and gold. The

8) _largest_ coral reef in the **9)** _world_ is the "Great

Barrier **10)** _Reef_" in Eastern Australia.

3. Missing Letters

In **Missing Letters** questions the cloze passage includes a number of words where letters have to be provided to complete the word.

Consonants and Vowels
It can be helpful to split up consonants and vowels when trying out various letters in spaces. Working through the alphabet is useful and does not take long.

Remember that:

- There are 21 consonants and some, such as **q**, **x** and **z**, are rarely used. This narrows it down to 18 regularly used consonants.
- There are five vowels: **a**, **e**, **i**, **o** and **u**.

Letter Combinations

Remember when doing missing letter questions that there are some rules that can help you identify missing letters:

- Certain consonants cannot be next to each other, e.g. **p** cannot be followed by **q** to make **pq**.
- Some same vowels cannot be next to each other, e.g. **u** cannot follow **u** to make **uu**.
- Some letters always go together, e.g. **qu**.
- Some vowels often go together, e.g. **ee**, **ea**, **ia**, etc.
- Some consonants often join together to form a different sound, e.g. **th** or **ph**.
- Most words begin with a consonant and end with a consonant, e.g. **boat**.
- A small number of words begin and end with a vowel, e.g. **era**.

Example: Fill in the missing letters to complete the passage below.

To make a cup of **1)** | t | | | , you boil the

2) | k | e | | t | | e | , put the teabag into the

3) | c | | p | , **4)** | p | | | r | in the water and

add **5)** | m | | | l | k | and sugar.

1. Read the passage carefully and decide what it is about. This passage is about making a cup of tea.

2. Look at the context of each word (words around it) and look for clues in the parts of speech:

   - 'To make a cup of [t| |]' - this word must be a noun and looking further on in the extract it mentions a teabag. It must be 'tea'.

   - 'you boil the [k|e| |t| |e]' – this word must be a noun. Looking for a letter pattern, [t|t|e] is a possibility as is [t|l|e]. The letters 'tle' are more likely so the answer must be 'kettle'.

   - 'put the teabag into the [c| | |p]' – this word must a be a noun. What would the teabag be put into? It must be a 'cup'.

   - '[p| | |r] in the water' – this word must be a verb. It must be 'pour' as water is poured.

   - '[m| | |l|k] and sugar' – a common addition to tea is milk, it must be 'milk'.

3. Read the passage to check all the missing letters that have been filled in make sensible words that fit the context. The passage will read:

To make a cup of **tea**, you boil the **kettle**, put the teabag into the **cup**, **pour** in the water and add **milk** and sugar.

The correct words are:
    1) tea   **2) kettle**   **3) cup**   **4) pour**   **5) milk**

a. Historical

Exercise 2: 6 Fill in the missing letters to complete the passage below:

The Battle of Hastings **1)** t o o k place on 14th October

1066. The **2)** b a t t l e was fought on a hill near a

3) v i l l a g e that is now **4)** k n o w n as

Battle, in East Sussex. The **5)** E n g l i s h army,

led by King Harold, took their position at the top of the hill. The

Norman **6)** a r m y , led by William the Conqueror,

7) p o s i t i o n e d themselves near the

8) b o t t o m of the hill. The fighting started in the

9) m o r n i n g and lasted all day. William won the

battle and was **10)** c r o w n e d King of England.

b. General Knowledge

Exercise 2: 7

Fill in the missing letters to complete the passage below:

Rainforests are very **1)** | t | | i | | k | , warm and wet forests.

They are found on **2)** | e | v | | r | | continent across the Earth,

except Antarctica. Rainforests get at **3)** | l | | | s | t | 250cm of

rain per year. Sometimes it is almost **4)** | d | | u | | l | e | that at

450cm. It can take ten **5)** | m | | n | | t | | s | for a falling rain

drop to **6)** | t | r | | v | | l | from the top of the rainforest to the

floor. The Amazon rainforest is the largest tropical rainforest in the

7) | w | o | | | d | . It is so big that if it were a country, it would be

the **8)** | n | | n | | h | biggest in the world. Rainforests only cover

six percent of the Earth's land **9)** | s | | r | f | | c | e | , but about

half of all **10)** | | n | | m | a | l | and plant species live there.

Chapter Three
SYNTAX

Syntax means arranging words and phrases to create well-formed sentences. Syntax questions usually involve unscrambling some jumbled words and forming them into a sentence.

Four things are helpful when forming correct sentences:

1. A sentence is a group of words that makes sense on its own. For example:

'Shoes, shirts, trousers, supermarket on Thursday' is not a sentence because it is incomplete. It is a list and a day and it is not clear what is meant.
'I drew a picture for my grandmother.' is a sentence because it is a complete statement.

2. A sentence should begin with a capital letter and end with a full stop. Sometimes these are included in questions to assist you when unscrambling a sentence.

3. A sentence should always include a verb (a doing word) and a subject (the thing or person doing the verb). It is important to look for these as it can help you reorder a sentence. For example:

*'The **children** (subject) **ate** (verb) their lunch at the cafe.'*

4. Sentences can contain two or more parts and can be separated by a conjunction or a preposition such as *'and'* or *'before'*. For example:

*'Vera collected three books from the library **and** laundry from the cleaners.'*

*'Vanessa went to breakfast club **before** she set off for school.'*

Syntax questions are of four types:

Words Changing Places • Basic Ordering

Selecting a Specific Word

Selecting the Extra Word

1. Words Changing Places

Example:

> Which two words have to change place to make this sentence read correctly?
>
> It is rain to going on Sunday.

1. Read the sentence and try and identify what it is about. This sentence seems to be about the weather.

2. Now look for the point in the sentence where it fails to make sense. The phrase 'rain to going' does not make sense as the verb would not be at the end. The words that need to change places are 'rain' and 'going'.

3. Check the words work in their new positions in the sentence.

'It is going to rain on Sunday.'

Exercise 3: 1

Underline the two words which should change place in order to make these sentences read correctly:

1) What is name your?

2) There are grey sky in the clouds.

3) pet has a She rabbit.

4) The park took the child to the parent.

5) He read the library from the book.

6) The football went to play brothers.

7) The picture painted the child.

8) The baked baker a cake.

9) raining has been It.

10) The snowman made a children.

Record scores out of ten here
↓

2. Basic Ordering

Example: | Unscramble the following sentence so that it makes complete sense:

tomorrow. my birthday It is

1. Check whether any of the words have a capital letter. This will show which word starts the sentence. 'It' does have a capital letter so this word begins the sentence. If there is no capital letter it is still important to find the word most likely to start the sentence.

2. Check whether any words have punctuation after them. This will show which word ends the sentence. The word 'tomorrow.' does have a full stop after it, so this word ends the sentence.

3. Think about the subject of the sentence as this may give some clues to forming a correct sentence. This sentence is about someone's birthday.

4. If this sentence begins with 'It', only 'is' can follow. This is likely to be followed with 'my birthday'.

5. Filling in the rest of the sentence is not very difficult. 'It is my birthday' must be followed by 'tomorrow'.

The correct sentence is:

'It is my birthday tomorrow.'

Exercise 3: 2   Unscramble the following words to form complete sentences:

1) Where post the office? is

_____

2) is Olly learning skateboard. to

_____

3) circus in The town. is

_____

4) child is a The ball. throwing

_____

5) car. Jamie with is a toy playing

_____

6) to how get you school do

_____

7) is making bird a the nest

_____

8) playing is Grace on trampoline the

_____

9) is Amanda on holiday going

_____

10) car my black is

_____ Score [ ]

3. Selecting a Specific Word

Example: | Unscramble and identify the fourth word in this sentence:

likes my brother swimming little

1. Read the scrambled sentence and try to identify what it is about. This sentence is obviously about a boy who likes swimming.

2. Identify which words must go together. There are two word combinations in this sentence; 'my little brother', and 'likes swimming'.

3. Now combine the phrases to make a sentence. This sentence would therefore read:

   'My little brother likes swimming.'

4. Look for the fourth word in the sentence:

   'My little brother likes swimming.'

   The fourth word in the sentence is: **likes**

Exercise 3: 3

Unscramble these words to make a sentence and underline the requested word:

Score

1) 6th word: family Spain is going to the

2) 1st word: I are hill to going Mum the walk and up

3) 4th word: do Ellie to lessons ballet wants

4) 2nd word: I sandwich a myself made ham

5) 5th word: driving test passed has her Shannon

6) 3rd word: Osman school to is walking

7) 2nd word: clowns very funny were the

8) 4th word: can piano play I the

9) 5th word: asleep my dog fallen has

10) 3rd word: is my the going sister to zoo

4. Selecting the Extra Word

Example: Unscramble these words to make a sentence and identify the one word which cannot fit into the sentence:

we having going a are party

1. Read the scrambled sentence and try to identify what it is about. As this sentence contains the noun 'party' it has something to do with a party.

2. Try to link words that are likely to go together. Focussing on the words 'we', 'having' and 'are' the phrase 'we are having' is possible. The sentence is likely to begin with this phrase.

3. Now try and build other words around the phrase, 'we are having'. The words 'party' and 'a' will obviously form 'a party'. The last part of the sentence must read: 'a party'.

4. The sentence would read: 'We are having a party'.

5. It is helpful to number the words to show the extra word, as follows:

1	3		4	2	5
we	having	**going**	a	are	party

Check for the word that is left over and cannot fit.

The word that will not fit into this sentence is: **going**

Score

Exercise 3: 4   Unscramble these words to make a sentence and underline the one extra word:

1) stop late was bus the

2) baked Tom cake cooked a

3) played piano good very the Sian well

4) of them all Hashaam exams passed his

5) out child the teacher corner room of sent the the

6) Mum up going is me to are after school pick

7) see family drove hours to Janet few many her for

8) I am of is scared spiders

9) boy likes basketball eating the playing

10) to need catch they train the Tuesday

Chapter Four
COMPREHENSION

Comprehension involves understanding a passage of text and answering questions about it.

This involves learning about the following:

Fiction & Non-fiction • Forms of Prose
Comprehension Skills • The Five Ws
The Three Question Types

1. Fiction & Non-fiction

Passages of text break into two basic categories:

- **Fiction** is text that is not true and has been created from a person's imagination.
- **Non-fiction** is text that is true and is based upon real events.

Example: Give an example of a piece of fiction.

The Tortoise never stopped for a moment, but went on with a slow but steady pace straight to the end of the course. The Hare, laid down and fell asleep. On waking up, he raced round the course, but found the Tortoise had crossed the finish line and was taking a nap.

This is fiction. It is an adapted extract from *The Hare and the Tortoise* by Aesop (620 to 560 BCE).

Example: Give an example of a piece of non-fiction.

Sir Walter Raleigh was an adventurer and was born in 1554 in Devon. He led many trips to America and introduced the potato to England. Raleigh was very close friends with Queen Elizabeth I.

This is non-fiction. It is an extract about *Sir Walter Raleigh*.

Exercise 4: 1

Identify whether these extracts of text are fiction or non-fiction:

1) *The rascal Brer Fox hated Brer Rabbit because he was always bossing everyone around. So, Brer Fox decided to catch and kill Brer Rabbit if it was the last thing he ever did! He thought carefully and came up with a cunning plan. He made a doll that looked like a baby. Then he stuck a hat on the doll and sat it in the middle of the road and waited for Brer Rabbit.*

Is this fiction or non-fiction? _____

2) *1st September 1664 - I heard my neighbours discuss that the plague had returned to Holland. It had begun in Amsterdam and Rotterdam, in 1663. Some said it came from Italy, others from Turkey or Cyprus by ship.*

Is this fiction or non-fiction? _____

3) *There was once an old castle, that stood in the middle of a deep, gloomy wood, and in the castle lived an old fairy. This fairy could take any shape she pleased. All day long she flew about in the form of an owl, or crept about the country like a cat; but at night she always became an old woman again.*

Is this fiction or non-fiction? _____

4) *"A monkey's paw?" said Mrs White with curiosity.*
"Yes, but it has magical powers," said the sergeant, casually.
His three listeners leaned forward eagerly. The sergeant put his empty glass to his lips and then put it down again. Mrs White filled the glass again for him.

Is this fiction or non-fiction? _____

5) *A python is a very large snake that lives in tropical parts of Africa, Asia and Australia. Pythons coil themselves around their prey and suffocate it, then swallow it whole.*

Is this fiction or non-fiction? _____

6) *One morning a little rabbit sat on a bank. He pricked his ears and listened to the trit-trot, trit-trot of a pony. A cart was coming along the road, driven by Mr McGregor and beside him sat Mrs McGregor in her best bonnet.*

Is this fiction or non-fiction? _____

7) *Henry VIII was born in 1491 and was famous for having six wives and making himself the head of the Church of England. He divorced Catherine of Aragon and Anne of Cleves. Anne Boleyn and Catherine Howard were beheaded. Jane Seymour died naturally and Catherine Parr outlived Henry who died in 1547.*

Is this fiction or non-fiction? _____

8) *A train is typically made up of an engine (called a locomotive) and carriages. Trains carry passengers or cargo along railway tracks. They are powered by electricity or diesel. The first steam locomotive was used to pull trucks of coal. It was invented by George Stephenson in 1825.*

Is this fiction or non-fiction? _____

9) *When the Rabbit actually took a watch out of its waistcoat-pocket, and looked at it, and then hurried on, Alice jumped to her feet. It flashed across her mind that she had never seen a rabbit before with either a waistcoat-pocket, or a watch to take out of it.*

Is this fiction or non-fiction? _____

10) *NEW YORK 12th October 1853 - My Dear Sister, I have not written to any of the family for some time. Firstly, I didn't know where they were, and secondly, I have been thinking about leaving New York every day for the last two weeks.*

Is this fiction or non-fiction? _____

2. Forms of Prose

Prose describes all forms of text that are not poetry. The basic categories forms of prose are as follows:

Narrative

This has a storyline with a beginning, middle and end. The events of the story are often based around a main character and sometimes a narrator tells the story. It is usually fictional but can be based on true events such as historical fiction. It includes novels, short stories, fables, legends, myths, fantasy and fairy stories.

This is an adapted extract of narrative text from *Facing the World* by Horatio Alger Jnr (1832-1899).

> *A mischievous idea came to Harry. In his village lived a man who had spent some time in the wild region beyond the Missouri River with the Native Americans. Harry had learned from him how to imitate the Native American war call.*
>
> *"I'll scare the old lady," thought Harry, smiling to himself. Immediately, there rang out from the bed, in the darkness and silence, a terrific war whoop from Harry. Mrs Fox was not normally nervous, but she jumped at the unexpected sound.*

Biography

This tells the story of someone's life. If somebody else tells their story it is called a biography.

This is a biographical extract about CS Lewis.

> *CS Lewis was born on 29th November 1898 in Northern Ireland. He was a writer and a professor at Oxford and Cambridge universities. His best-known books are The Chronicles of Narnia, a series of seven fantasy books. He died in Cambridge on 22nd November 1963, aged 64.*

Factual Text

This kind of text contains truthful information without giving an opinion. It can include textbooks, encyclopedias, leaflets, recipes, catalogues, directories and manuals.

This is a piece of factual text about *Vikings*.

> *The Vikings are also called Norsemen, and came from Scandinavia. They travelled over the sea in longships, which are long, narrow wooden boats. Vikings first attacked Britain in 787CE looking for farm land to live on.*

Letters or Emails

These are a form of communication from one person or group to another. They can be formal (a letter of complaint) or informal (a personal letter to a friend). Text messages are another way of communicating using prose.

This is an extract of a letter from Simon to Liam.

> *Dear Liam,*
> *It was nice to receive your letter. I am well and I am glad to hear you are too. I have been busy recently but hope to visit you soon.*
> *Best wishes,*
> *Simon.*

Journals or Diaries

These are a way of recording daily events or personal experiences. They often include a date or time of day for each entry and can include very personal information and thoughts. Journals are normally more detailed than diaries.

This is an extract from *The Diary of a Girl in France in 1821* by Mary Browne (1807-1833).

> *April 25th, 1821 — We arrived in London about eleven o'clock. All the hotels we enquired at were full. We drove to the British Hotel on Jermyn Street, Piccadilly. We passed through Cavendish Square, which was very pretty, but I was rather disappointed at not seeing all of London.*

Example: | Identify the form of prose below. |

Amelia Earhart was born on 24th July 1897 in Kansas. She is best known for being the first woman to fly over the Atlantic Ocean. She disappeared on 2nd July 1937 over the Pacific Ocean. She was declared dead on 5th January 1939.

Answer: This form of prose is biographical as it is about the pilot Amelia Earhart's life.

Exercise 4: 2

Identify the form of prose in the following extracts:

Score

1) *Once upon a time there were three little kittens, and their names were Mittens, Tom Kitten and Moppet. They had dear little fur coats of their own; and they tumbled about the doorstep and played in the dust.*

   This form of prose is _____.

2) *Neil Armstrong is famous for being the first human to walk on the moon. This historic moment happened on 20th July 1969. As he stepped onto the moon, he said these famous words, "That's one small step for man, one giant leap for mankind."*

   This form of prose is _____.

3) *11th April — Today was very annoying. I was late for an appointment having missed the quarter-to-nine bus to the city. This was because I had a disagreement with the boy who delivers the groceries. He came straight into the house without asking, and left dirty boot marks all over the carpet. I hope that tomorrow will be a better day.*

   This form of prose is _____.

4) *A pony is a small breed of horse. Sometimes they are no larger than 13 hands in height, but they are never more than 14 hands tall (a hand is a unit of measurement that is 4 inches or 10cm).*

   This form of prose is _____.

5) *Dear Santa,*

   I have been really good this year. For Christmas I would like a doll and a games console. Thank you.

   From, Sophie. (age 7)

   This form of prose is _____.

6) *A drum is a percussion instrument that makes noise by being hit with either hands or sticks. Drums are used in various types of musical ensembles, such as, orchestras, marching bands and pop groups.*

   This form of prose is _____.

7) *We were always ready for tea at any time, and especially when combined with beasts. There was marmalade, too, and apricot jam, brought in especially for us; and afterwards the beast-book was spread out, and, as the man had truly said, it contained every sort of beast that had ever been in the world.*

   This form of prose is _____.

8) *To Myriam,*

   The weather is great here in Spain. I am having a lovely time going to the beach and playing in the swimming pool.

   Wish you were here,

   Paula.

   This form of prose is _____.

9) *Florence Nightingale was born on 12th May 1820. She was known as the Lady of the Lamp because she often carried a lamp when caring for sick soldiers during the Crimean War (1853-1856). She was the first woman to receive the Order of Merit.*

   This form of prose is _____.

10) *12th July 1919 - Hella and I are writing everything down. We both agreed that when we went to the high school we would do this every day. Dora keeps a diary too, but she gets furious if I look at it. I call Helene "Hella," and she calls me "Rita."*

   This form of prose is _____.

3. Comprehension Skills

When first looking at a passage of text, always remember to:

- **Read Without 'Voicing'** - This means to read the passage by silently 'mouthing the text' without using your voice. This helps concentration when reading and stops the mind from wandering.

- **Read Actively** - When reading look for information in the text that will give clues to what it is about.

- **Answer Correctly** - Read the multiple-choice answer options very carefully before selecting an answer.

It is then possible to scan the text. This means to quickly look through the text without reading everything in detail in order to find the answers.

4. The Four Ws

Four basic questions can be asked to explore information contained in the text:

1. **Where does it take place?** Look out for the locations that are mentioned in the text and how they are described.

2. **When does it take place?** In what period of history is the passage set? Are there any other clues about the time of day, year, season, or how long any action takes place for?

3. **Who is involved?** Identify any key characters and look for descriptions of them.

4. **What happens?** Look for the main actions that occur in the passage. Is there one key event?

Example: Read the following passage about Colombus and answer the four 'w' questions:

1) Where does it take place?
2) When does it take place?
3) Who is involved?
4) What happens?

About 500 years ago, the world was still being explored.

Christopher Columbus, an Italian explorer, was born in 1451. On 3rd August 1492, he sailed from Europe and bravely crossed the Atlantic Ocean, not knowing where he would land. He had three wooden sailing ships and 90 men. In the ships' holds they stored salted fish in barrels, cheese, wine, water, live pigs and chickens.

The journey took longer than expected. There was no land, just ocean. The men became frightened because they were running out of food and water, but Columbus would not give up.

After 36 days, the sailors spotted an island. The sea was crystal clear and the land was full of fruit and greenery. On 12th October 1492, Columbus went ashore, knelt, kissed the earth and tearfully thanked God. He called the island San Salvador. It was in the Bahamas.

1) Where does it take place?

List the locations mentioned - Europe, the Atlantic Ocean, San Salvador in the Bahamas and three wooden ships.

Note any descriptions given - San Salvador is described as fruitful and green with clear seas.

2) When does it take place?

Note the period of history - About 500 years ago, in the 1400s.

List any specific dates or time periods - Columbus was born in 1451. He set sail from Europe on 3rd August 1492. He landed on San Salvador on 12th October 1492.

3) Who is involved?

List the key characters - The passage is mainly about Christopher Columbus. His crew of 90 men are mentioned.

Describe the main features of the characters - The men were brave explorers but they did become frightened. Columbus would not allow them to give up.

4) What happens?

List the main events - Columbus and his men made a 36-day journey from Europe to San Salvador and landed safely.

What is the main event that takes place? The arrival on the island and the naming of San Salvador by Columbus.

Exercise 4: 3

Read the following passage, *King of the Birds*, and answer the following questions:

Score

One day the birds decided that one of them must be made king. The birds from the woods and fields assembled on a beautiful May morning. Among their number was the eagle, the robin, the bluebird, the owl, the lark, the cuckoo, the lapwing and the (4) *sparrow. There was also a very small nameless bird. After much confusion, piping, hissing, chattering and clacking, they decided that the bird that could fly highest should be king.*

There was loud rustling, whirring and beating of wings and the air (8) *was full of dust. All at once the birds flew in a great flock like a black cloud floating over the field. The little birds soon grew tired and fell back to earth. The larger ones held out longer, flew higher, but the eagle flew the highest. He rose up until he seemed to be* (12) *flying into the sun. More birds gave up and returned to earth.*

The eagle thought to himself, 'What's the use of flying higher? It's settled: I'm king!'

The birds called: "Come down! You're our king! No one can (16) fly higher than you."

"Except me!" cried a shrill voice, and the nameless little bird rose up from the eagle's back, where he had hidden in the feathers. (20)

He mounted up until he was lost to sight, then, folded his wings and sank to earth crying, "I'm king!"

"You, our king!" the birds cried angrily; "you've done this by trickery. We'll not let you reign over us." (24)

The birds gathered again and made another condition, that the new king must go the deepest into the earth. The goose wallowed in the sand and the duck attempted to dig a hole! Other birds tried to hide themselves in the ground, but the nameless little bird found (28) a mouse's hole, and crept in.

He cried: "I'm king!"

"You, our king!" the birds protested, even more angrily.

"Do you think we would reward you for your cunning? No! (32) You'll stay in the earth until you die of hunger!"

They shut up the little bird in the mouse's hole, and told the owl watch him carefully night and day. Then the birds went home to bed, for they were tired. The owl became lonely and weary just (36) staring at the mouse's hole. 'I'll close one eye and watch with the other,' he thought. He stared with his open eye but was soon fast asleep.

The nameless little bird peeped out, and when he saw the Owl (40) asleep, he slipped from the hole and flew away. The owl dared not show himself by day lest the birds should pull him to pieces. He flies about only at night-time, pursuing the mouse who made the hole in which the little bird crept. (44)

The little bird also keeps out of sight, for he fears the other birds might punish him for his cleverness.

He hides in hedges, and when he thinks he is safe, he sings out, "I'm king!" (48)

And the other birds mock him, "Yes, the hedge-king!"

Adapted from the story by The Brothers Grimm (1785-1863).

Where

1) During the first challenge, where did it look like the eagle was heading?

- ☐ a) To the top of a mountain
- ☐ b) Towards home
- ☑ c) Towards the sun
- ☐ d) Down to the earth

2) Where does the little bird hide last of all?

- ☐ a) In the mouse's hole
- ☑ b) In hedges
- ☐ c) In a nest
- ☐ d) In the sky

When

3) In what season is the passage set?

- ☐ a) Spring
- ☑ b) Summer
- ☐ c) Autumn
- ☐ d) Winter

4) At what time of day does the owl take flight towards the end of the passage?

- ☐ a) At dawn
- ☐ b) During the day
- ☐ c) At dusk
- ☑ d) At night

Who

5) Who flew highest in line 12?

- ☑ a) The eagle
- ☐ b) The bluebird
- ☐ c) The robin
- ☐ d) The lapwing

6) Which bird attempted to dig a hole?

    ☐ a) The cuckoo
    ☐ b) The sparrow
    ☑ c) The goose
    ☐ d) The duck

7) Who was told to watch over the nameless bird?

    ☐ a) The eagle
    ☐ b) The robin
    ☐ c) The mouse
    ☑ d) The owl

What

8) What 'trickery' did the nameless bird use to win the first challenge?

    ☐ a) It climbed a tree
    ☐ b) It waited at the bottom
    ☑ c) It hid in the eagle's feathers
    ☐ d) It hid in the dust

9) What did the nameless bird do to become king in the second challenge?

    ☐ a) It wallowed in sand
    ☑ b) It crept into a mouse's hole
    ☐ c) It dug a hole
    ☐ d) It hid in the ground

10) What did the owl do while watching the mouse's hole?

    ☐ a) It hunted
    ☐ b) It went home
    ☑ c) It fell asleep
    ☐ d) It flew away

5. The Two Question Types

There are two types of comprehension question. They are as follows:

- **Factual Information** – This involves finding straightforward facts from the text. It is sometimes described as finding information 'on the line'.

- **Contextual Understanding** – This requires understanding what comes before and after the relevant part of the text. The answer is not always obvious. This is often called finding the answer 'between the lines'.

Example: Read the following passage about *Castles* and answer these two questions:

1) Why did they start to use stone to build castles? (Factual)

2) Why did castles have moats? (Contextual)

Castles were built during the Middle Ages for kings, princes and lords. They would rule the local people who farmed the land surrounding the castle. The first castles were made of wood, but later they were replaced with stone to make them stronger. Castles were easy to defend from attack and were often built at the top of hills. (4)

They usually had a moat which was a ditch dug around the castle filled with water. A drawbridge could be lowered across the moat to enter the castle gate. The gatehouse was built at the gate to help reinforce the castle defences at its weakest point. The keep was a large tower in the centre of the castle. The castle wall had a walkway on it and slits in the walls from where archers could fire arrows at attackers. (8) (12)

1) **Why did they start to use stone to build castles?**

   The answer to this question can be found easily in the text. The passage says castles were first built of wood and later stone was used to make them stronger.

2) **Why did castles have moats?**

   This question is a little more difficult because it involves understanding the text. Castles had moats to stop people climbing the castle walls or entering the gatehouse.

Exercise 4: 4

Read the following passage, *Cinderella*, and answer the following questions:

Arabella lived happily with her loving parents, Grenville and Gertrude. When she was nine, her mother fell sick.

She called Arabella, "Always be good, my child; be patient whatever happens, and even if you experience difficult times, you'll only find happiness if you're well-behaved." (4)
Then Gertrude died and Arabella wept.

Grenville was so lonely he searched for a new wife who could be a stepmother to Arabella. His choice was a proud and bossy (8)
widow with a cruel temper called Hagatha. She already had two daughters, Edna and Beryl, who were just as bad-tempered and thought they were better than others.

As soon as Hagatha moved in, she treated Arabella badly. (12)
Arabella's gentle personality was so different to the selfish and nasty behaviour of her stepsisters. Hagatha made Arabella wash all the dishes, scrub the stairs and polish the floors. Arabella slept on a straw mattress in a cold attic and ate scraps. However, (16)
Edna and Beryl slept on feather beds in beautiful rooms and were served fancy dishes. Arabella only put up with it because she did not want to upset Grenville who respected his new wife.

When Arabella finished working, she often sat near the fireplace (20)
to warm herself. Hagatha did not like using Arabella's name

because it sounded too friendly. As Arabella sat among the cinders, Hagatha decided to join 'cinder' with 'bella' and named her Cinderella. (24)

Although Cinderella dressed shabbily, her simple beauty made her far more attractive than her overdressed stepsisters. They covered their faces with ugly makeup and always complained. Cinderella often felt sad and missed her real mother. (28)

One day, the king's son gave a ball and invited all the important people. The stepsisters spent days choosing outfits. Cinderella was forced to iron and sew their dresses.

    Edna, the eldest said, "I'll put on my red velvet dress with (32) *lace trimmings" while Beryl, not to be outdone, boasted, "I'll wear a golden satin gown with a diamond necklace."*

While her stepsisters prepared for the ball, Cinderella cried by the fireplace. As she stared at the flames, her mother's ghostly face (36) *appeared.*

    Gertrude's voice seemed to echo across the kitchen, "This night, your rags will become rich silk, your shoes, red leather and you'll travel to the ball in a golden coach. On the stroke of (40) *midnight all will be as before."*

Suddenly, Cinderella transformed into a beautiful princess, just as Gertrude had said and the coach waited outside. Cinderella arrived at the ball and her stepsisters did not recognise her. (44) *At nearly midnight, the prince asked her to dance. As soon as Cinderella heard the clock strike twelve she rushed from the ballroom, but accidentally left one shoe behind.*

For days, the prince searched the kingdom for the owner of (48) *the lost shoe. Eventually, he arrived, with his courtiers, at Cinderella's house. Edna and Beryl tried to force their feet into the red shoe without success. To their horror, Cinderella tried the shoe and it fitted. The prince asked Cinderella to marry him* (52) *immediately.*

<u>Notes on text:</u>
Widow (line 11) – a woman whose husband has died

Factual Information

1) How old was Arabella when Gertrude died?

- [ ] a) Eight
- [ ] b) Nine
- [ ] c) Ten
- [ ] d) Eleven

2) Which of these daily chores is not mentioned in the passage?

- [ ] a) Washing the dishes
- [ ] b) Scrubbing the stairs
- [ ] c) Polishing the floors
- [ ] d) Cooking the dinner

3) Where did Hagatha get the idea for the name 'Cinderella'?

- [ ] a) Arabella sitting among the cinders
- [ ] b) Arabella sleeping on a straw mattress
- [ ] c) Arabella cleaning the fireplace
- [ ] d) Arabella eating scraps

4) Which of these best describes Cinderella?

- [ ] a) Proud
- [ ] b) Selfish
- [ ] c) Gentle
- [ ] d) Nasty

5) What time did Cinderella leave the ball?

- [ ] a) Midnight
- [ ] b) 8 o'clock
- [ ] c) 6 o'clock
- [ ] d) Noon

Contextual Understanding

6) Why did Edna and Beryl think they were better than others?

☐ a) They were Hagatha's real daughters
☐ b) They went through difficult times
☐ c) They were bad-tempered
☐ d) Grenville liked them more than Cinderella

7) What does the word 'outdone' (line 33) mean in this passage?

☐ a) Lose
☐ b) Done well
☐ c) Beaten
☐ d) Outburst

8) What material was Cinderella's dress made from?

☐ a) Velvet
☐ b) Satin
☐ c) Gold
☐ d) Silk

9) Why did her stepsisters not recognise Cinderella?

☐ a) She was working at the ball
☐ b) Her appearance had changed
☐ c) She could dance
☐ d) She had been crying

10) Why did the prince look for the owner of the lost shoe?

☐ a) He wanted to return the shoe
☐ b) He wanted to find a wife
☐ c) He wanted to dance with the owner
☐ d) He wanted to meet the family of the owner

Score

Notes

Answers

Chapter One
Classification

Exercise 1: 1
1) trousers
2) aunt
3) chicken
4) oak
5) hotel
6) ball
7) London
8) teacher
9) yoghurt
10) paper

Exercise 1: 2
1) allow
2) seagull
3) rear
4) right
5) join
6) shovel
7) met
8) him
9) slate
10) man

Exercise 1: 3
1) size
2) good
3) calm
4) frown
5) close
6) fine
7) new
8) great
9) nice
10) glad

Exercise 1: 4
1) sad
2) pink
3) sky
4) outside
5) bellow
6) Sun
7) cry
8) water
9) thin
10) meat

Exercise 1: 5
1) start
2) hide
3) stone
4) relax
5) sofa
6) plus
7) shady
8) smile
9) caring
10) dirty

Exercise 1: 6
1) pole
2) narrow
3) empty
4) scared
5) remain
6) rabbit
7) right
8) beach
9) chilly
10) every

Exercise 1: 7
1) close
2) beautiful
3) bang
4) every
5) centre
6) silent
7) helpful
8) quick
9) hurry
10) fantastic

Exercise 1: 8
1) whisper
2) well
3) girl
4) over
5) dirty
6) West
7) low
8) after
9) laugh
10) fail

Exercise 1: 9
1) light
2) subtract
3) little
4) speak
5) dead
6) better
7) early
8) upset
9) true
10) everything

Answers

Exercise 1: 10
1) left
2) first
3) outside
4) loud
5) weak
6) leave
7) closed
8) night
9) cooked
10) start

Exercise 1: 11
1) arms
2) ball
3) bark
4) bow
5) tear
6) fast
7) band
8) second
9) flag
10) box

Chapter Two
Cloze
Exercise 2: 1
1) yesterday, loud, light
2) circus, funny, water
3) name, clock, England
4) filling, slices, eaten
5) child, ill, doctor
6) pirate, map, treasure
7) rain, train, delays
8) kite, large, prey
9) highest, located, above
10) fictional, children, princess

Exercise 2: 2
1) again
2) too
3) said
4) sooner
5) proud
6) big
7) see
8) working
9) began
10) going

Exercise 2: 3
1) known
2) learnt
3) steam
4) working
5) write
6) after
7) first
8) best
9) train
10) faster

Exercise 2: 4
1) boat
2) middle
3) sink
4) fish
5) narrow
6) courage
7) lay
8) full
9) swam
10) still

Exercise 2: 5
1) country
2) six
3) two
4) city
5) many
6) capital
7) colours
8) largest
9) world
10) Reef

Exercise 2: 6
1) took
2) battle
3) village
4) known
5) English
6) army
7) positioned
8) bottom
9) morning
10) crowned

Exercise 2: 7
1) thick
2) every
3) least
4) double
5) minutes
6) travel
7) world
8) ninth
9) surface
10) animal

Answers

Chapter Three
Syntax

Exercise 3: 1
1) name & your
2) sky & clouds
3) pet & She
4) park & parent
5) library & book
6) football & brothers
7) picture & child
8) baked & baker
9) raining & It
10) snowman & children

Exercise 3: 2
1) Where is the post office?
2) Olly is learning to skateboard.
3) The circus is in town.
4) The child is throwing a ball.
5) Jamie is playing with a toy car.
6) How do you get to school?
7) The bird is making a nest.
8) Grace is playing on the trampoline.
9) Amanda is going on holiday.
10) My car is black.

Exercise 3: 3
1) Spain
2) Mum
3) do
4) made
5) driving
6) walking
7) clowns
8) the
9) asleep
10) is

Exercise 3: 4
1) stop
2) cooked
3) good
4) them
5) corner
6) are
7) few
8) is
9) eating
10) Tuesday

Chapter Four
Comprehension

Exercise 4: 1
1) Fiction - An adapted extract from Brer Rabbit by Joel Chandler Harris (1848-1908)
2) Non-fiction - Adapted from A Journal of the Plague Year by Daniel Defoe (1660-1731)
3) Fiction - An adapted extract from Jorinda And Jorindel, Fairy Tales by The Brothers Grimm (1785-1863)
4) Fiction - An adapted extract from The Monkey's Paw by WW Jacobs (1863-1943)
5) Non-fiction - An extract about pythons
6) Fiction - An adapted extract from The Tale of Benjamin Bunny by Beatrix Potter (1866-1943)
7) Non-fiction - An extract about Henry VIII
8) Non-fiction - An extract about trains

Answers

9) Fiction - An adapted extract from Alice's Adventures in Wonderland by Lewis Carroll (1832-1898)

10) Non-fiction - A letter to Miss Moffet from Mark Twain (1835-1910)

Exercise 4: 2

1) Narrative - An adapted extract from The Tale of Tom Kitten by Beatrix Potter (1866-1943).

2) Biography - an extract about Neil Armstrong

3) Journal or Diary - An adapted extract from The Diary of a Nobody by George Grossmith and Weedon Grossmith (1847-1917)

4) Factual - an extract about ponies

5) Letter or E-mail - a letter to Santa

6) Factual - an extract about drums

7) Narrative - an adapted extract from The Reluctant Dragon by Kenneth Grahame (1859-1932)

8) Letter or E-mail - a letter from holiday

9) Biography - An extract about Florence Nightingale

10) Journal or Diary - an extract from A Young Girl's Diary by Anonymous

Exercise 4: 3

1) c
2) b
3) a
4) d
5) a
6) d
7) d
8) c
9) b
10) c

Exercise 4: 4

1) b
2) d
3) a
4) c
5) a
6) a
7) c
8) d
9) b
10) b

PROGRESS CHARTS

Shade in your score for each exercise on the graph. Add up for your total score.

1. CLASSIFICATION

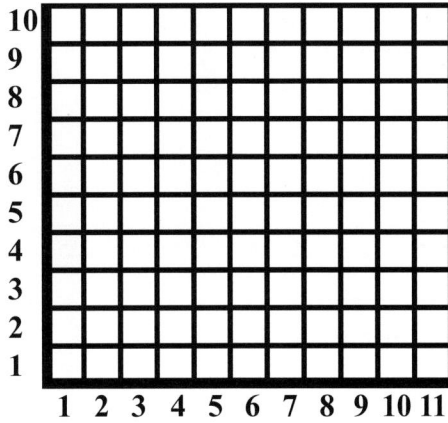

Scores

Total Score

Percentage %

Exercises

2. CLOZE

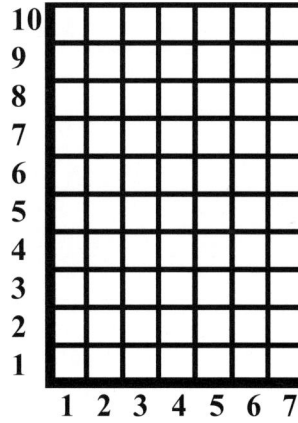

Scores

Total Score

Percentage %

Exercises

3. SYNTAX

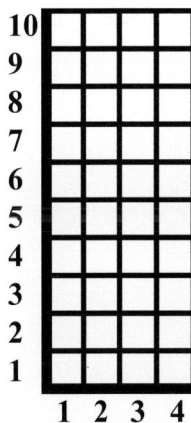

Scores

Total Score

Percentage %

Exercises

4. COMPREHENSION

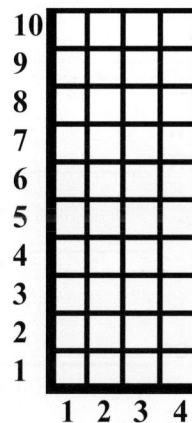

Scores

Total Score

Percentage %

Exercises

Add up the percentages and divide by 4

Overall
Percentage   %

CERTIFICATE OF

ACHIEVEMENT

This certifies

_____

has successfully completed

11+ Verbal Reasoning
Year 3/4 CEM Style
WORKBOOK **1**

Overall percentage
score achieved

%

Comment _____

_____

Signed _____
(teacher/parent/guardian)

Date _____

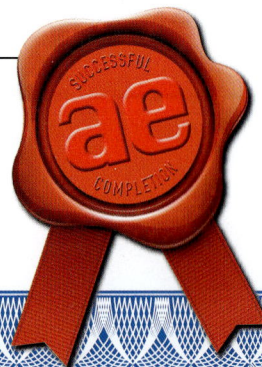